WATCH IT!

WATCH IT!

The Use of Body Language in Word of Mouth Advertising

Godfrey Harris

Viva Books Private Limited

New Delhi • Mumbai • Chennai • Kolkata • Bangalore • Hyderabad

First Indian Edition 2005

VIVA BOOKS PRIVATE LIMITED

- 4262/3 Ansari Road, Daryaganj, New Delhi 110 002
  E-mail: viva@vivagroupindia.net
- 215-216 New Apollo Estate, 2nd Floor, Mogra Lane, Andheri (E), Mumbai 400 069
  E-mail: vivamumbai@vivagroupindia.net
- Jamals Fazal Chambers, 26 Greams Road, Chennai 600 006
  E-mail: vivachennai@vivagroupindia.net
- B-103, Jindal Towers, 21/1A/3, Darga Road, Kolkata 700 017
  E-mail: vivakolkata@vivagroupindia.net
- 7 GF, Sovereign Park Apartments, 56-58 K.R. Road, Basavanagudi, Bangalore 560 004
  Email: vivabangalore@vivagroupindia.net
- 101 & 102, Mughal Marc Apartments, Narayanguda, Hyderabad 500 029
  Email: vivahyderabad@vivagroupindia.net

Published by arrangement with

The Americas Group
9200 Sunset Blvd., Suite 404
Los Angeles, California 90069-3506
USA.

ISBN 81-309-0037-8

Published by Vinod Vasishtha for Viva Books Private Limited, 4262/3 Ansari Road, Daryaganj, New Delhi 110 002. and printed & bound at Raj Press, R-3 Inderpuri, New Delhi - 110 012.

TABLE OF CONTENTS

INTRODUCTION

INTRODUCTION

This is the third book in a series we began a few years ago to explore all of the skills that can make word of mouth advertising as effective as possible in the marketplace.

The first book, *Don't Take Our Word For It!*, set the stage. It offered a comprehensive discussion of word of mouth concepts and implementable programs that can stimulate satisfied customers into talking with their own contacts about products, services, places, and events they have experienced. The second book, *Talk Is Easy*, was designed to make every conversation about a product, service, place, or event payoff in some way. In fact, the goal was to offer simple-to-remember techniques that could make every conversation as fluid as a river flowing toward the ocean.

The back cover of that book featured the following mock newspaper article from something we called "Modern Marketing News":

> *Los Angeles, CA (Special)—To a lot of people, making conversation with a stranger is about as scary as meeting their potential in-laws for the first time. How do you get beyond the how-do-you-do stage? How do you know what to say to someone you've never met before? How do you change the subject when a conversation gets so boring you feel you're about to fall asleep?*
>
> *All good questions that are answered in the pages of* Talk Is Easy. *By the time a small-business owner, corporate salesperson, network marketer, or anyone else finishes*

> *this book, they should be able to have a conversation with a member of the Royal Family or a member of the Royal Mounted Police—whether they are alone with them in a room or standing in a crowd at an airport, whether the subject is financial matters or family matters.*

The imaginary article went on to state our firm belief that any person who can change his or her age once a year or can change lanes on a highway in a car can learn how to make conversation with anyone at any time in any situation. The secret, we believe, is remembering a few simple rules on conversational techniques.

This is the third book in the same word of mouth series. *Watch It!* explores an equally important skill—how to read and use body language when words are not the only, or perhaps even the best, way to convey a message or express a point of view. We employ the same basic approach here that we used in the book on conversation: We provide an example of how some element of body language has been described or has come into our own experience, extract a principle or rule about body language that leads from that example, and suggest some ways to practice doing or recognizing an element of body language to fix it in the mind.

Our purpose is to help individuals and businesspeople recognize the meaning of body language and/or use body language to improve their ability to communicate. Specifically, we are most interested in exploring ways to use body language to enhance the impact of word of mouth advertising. By now, many of our readers know we hold that word of mouth advertising is equal as a promotional form to traditional media advertising, public relations, and product presentation. In fact, we believe that it may soon become the preferred method of promotion as e-commerce becomes an even more important factor in marketing. Why?

Because many in the public have finally come to recognize what seems to be the pervasive corruption in the other forms of promotion. Traditional media advertising often fails to tell people who are not likely to benefit from a product; public relations is universally bought and paid for by the very individual or company being promoted by the PR firm; and product presentations always package their items in the most favorable possible light. The judgments of friends, relatives, and associates, on the other hand, are trusted because they have no reason to embellish the truth and no conflict of interest to taint their viewpoints.

But as we always point out, word of mouth is not automatic; even close relations and good friends seldom speak about their mouthwash or brand of motor oil without some form of prompting. As a result, every business needs to have at least one program in place to help their current customers speak about their products and services to others.

These programs, we find, are enhanced by the use of body language. A person's posture, tone of voice, and enthusiasm when using a product, offering a sample, or describing a service often convey far more than words on their own.

We hope you learn how to use and interpret body language as a result of reading this volume and we hope you will incorporate body language into your future word of mouth programs. Most of all, though, we hope you have fun in the process.

Godfrey Harris

Los Angeles, California
May 2001

RULES OF THE ROAD

RULES OF THE ROAD

The man in the rumpled suit edged up to the open door and leaned heavily against the wall. The uniformed policeman nodded to him and moved slightly to the left so as not to obscure the suit's view into the room. The man clearly wanted to see what was happening inside without being observed himself. Not that he had to worry very much. The woman he wanted to watch was constantly dabbing at her eyes with a tissue while obsessively smoothing out her skirt as she crossed and uncrossed what must have been the longest pair of legs in the highest pair of heels on the planet.

That's one good-looking woman, he thought. Can it be that she is really in her mid fifties as the tabloids say? Occasionally, the man noticed that she would look up to glance at the activity around her without really seeming to see anything that was going on. At these moments, he noticed that there wasn't a line on her face to detract from those gorgeous green eyes and the luster of her famously tousled mane of brunette hair.

After staring for a good 30 seconds at how she was dressed and how she moved, the man in the suit turned his attention to the forensic specialists from the police department. They were moving incessantly around the room—inspecting marks on the wall, measuring distances, dusting a powdery material over the light switches, snipping fragments of carpet, laying out numbered cards.

A totally separate group of people was hovering over a mound on the floor to the left. The mound had the shape of a human form; the mound didn't move. The group, however, was urgently conferring about something and pointing at various objects, as if they hoped the inert shape could provide information for whatever they were discussing.

As the man in the suit continued to survey the scene in the room, he heard the motor drive of an automatic camera. Before he could locate the police photographer, he instinctively knew that some 10 to 15 images had been recorded. He also knew the numbers didn't matter; everything in that room would be shot from every conceivable angle for later study.

While all of this was going on, another young police officer approached the lady on the couch, notebook in hand. As he began to ask her questions between her sobs, the man in the suit stepped through the doorway and moved toward the two people, introducing himself as he approached:

"Mrs. Finestead, I'm Detective Steel."

She looked up. She seemed confused and scared all at the same time. Was this acting or genuine emotion? he wondered. He couldn't tell. She crossed her legs one more time. Then she quickly uncrossed them again, primly setting her feet together flat on the floor. Next she returned to carefully smoothing out the wrinkles in her skirt and flicking at her hair to get it out of her eyes. Detective Steel continued.

"We are all naturally very sorry to learn what happened to the Lieutenant Governor here tonight. As you know, he was a good friend of every police department in the state. And he was hated by all the bad guys. But we have to find out exactly what happened. So I am sure you won't mind answering Officer Norris's questions. When he finishes, I may have some additional ones for you as well. Go ahead, Chris..."

Officer Norris resumed his basic questions in no special order:

- Was Lieutenant Governor Andrews acting normally when you last talked to him?
- When did you arrive here this evening?
- Did you know whether he planned to meet anyone else tonight?

Detective Steel stood back to listen to Mrs. Finestead's responses while continuing to watch her movements closely. Another suit arrived. This one was all tight creases and carefully coiffed grey hair. He seemed poised to ask questions if either Officer Norris or Detective Steel left an opening. Mrs. Finestead glanced up to see him. Her expression froze.

"CUT!"

"Let's save it."

"Terrific work everyone. Take five while we set up the next shot."

The scene just described encompasses moments from different television programs, black-and-white movies, and old stage plays we've all seen a dozen times. Here was the grisly death of a prominent politician, a beautiful grieving friend with a questionable relationship to the deceased, multiple potential motives forming for the murder, and a number of possible alibis. The audience comes to realize that the authorities have a host of nagging doubts and the rest of the program / film / play will be spent trying to fill in the holes and evaluate the evidence to determine the perpetrator of the crime.

As these types of stories unfold, you know the questions about the vehemently professed innocence of the beautiful grieving friend will be thoroughly analyzed. While the basic story may seem so unassailable, something keeps a mythical detective like Steel wondering and probing and searching.

It is usually nothing a Mrs. Finestead-type has said—nothing she claims—just the way she acts when she talks. Is it how she sits? The way she touches her skirt? The tone in her voice? The rhythm she develops when she nervously flicks at her hair? Something is clearly making the detective uneasy, but putting his finger on what it is in the context of everything else he knows about this case at this time has not yet come into focus.

Welcome to the fascinating topic of body language—those nonverbal gestures, movements, and voice cues that convey what someone really *means* and what he or she actually *feels* at this precise moment without using specific words to express the same information.

Perhaps the best example of the power and impact of body language involves a variation of a skit from vaudeville days. As the actor sits in a chair pretending to be reading a newspaper, a female voice sounds offstage. She asks him in a plaintive voice:

"Don't you miss having a different woman every time you are in a different city?"

"NOOOOO, my love," he booms at the audience, "not since you've come into my life."

But as he says that famous line with all the cheer of a sailor on shore leave, he looks around the edge of his newspaper to nod his head up and down. The audience can see a wry smile curl around his lips and realizes that the *words* he has just spoken are not as indicative of his true feelings as the facial expression and head movement he is making. All of us have seen this little skit…and we all know that when we see it, we accept the fact that the man's body language represents the truth far more than the words he is speaking.

Of course, not all body language conveys such clean and clear responses as happens on stage in that skit. Sometimes body language is much more ambiguous.

Take for example the fact that some believe people who rub their noses as they answer a question are really subconsciously signaling that their response is untrue. It is sometimes called the Pinocchio effect. Now, there may even be some scientific truth behind the famous Italian fairy tale. University researchers have recently said that their studies demonstrate that untruths actually change hormonal balances and blood flow. The added flows enlarge blood vessels in the nose, which in turn creates an itching sensation. People spotted rubbing their nose while denying knowledge of something important may be giving away the fact that their blood vessels are expanding and that they are actually fibbing.

Those caught rubbing their nose in midresponse will argue that it is merely a coincidence or that they had a genuine itch caused by an insect bite or rash. Could be, of course. But can you be sure?

You can't. As with any other piece of information flowing to your various receptors, you need to take the nose rubbing into account as you assess its value in terms of all the other signals you are getting to decide any issue. This book is about making you a body language detective—someone who can interpret movements and gestures and/or use them with sufficient confidence to understand or convey the truth of what is being discussed. We can't make you an expert, but we can make you comfortable with interpreting a form of communication that arose in animals long before the ability to *speak* arose with humans.

To keep your sleuthing consistent, think of the Spanish word for "hello." As many of you know, it is *hola,* pronounced with the "h" silent. The rest of the letters and their proper pronunciation—OLA—become a perfect acronym for dealing with body language. From now on, when you see repeated gestures, odd movements, strange mannerisms, or unconventional accessories, think OLA:

- *Observe*
- *Link*
- *Analyze*

O-L-A. Simple to remember and simple to execute. Here's how it works:

O *Observe* the body language closely. Does it seem to be expressing the person's real feelings or thoughts at that moment rather than reflecting some physical problem or involuntary reaction?

L *Link* the body language observed to the words being expressed—do they match, does one form of communication reinforce the other, or is their some type of discord between them?

A *Analyze* the words and body language together to try to determine what is really being conveyed by the individual.

To review: First *observe* the gesture, movement, or mannerism, then*link* it to the words being spoken, and finally *analyze* the full meaning of what is being communicated.

Watching body language is one thing. We also want you to learn the other side—how to *use* it to add impact, emphasis, and meaning to what *you* are conveying to someone else. It is also important for you to recognize when you may be giving off the wrong signals—saying and meaning one thing but showing body language that conveys something entirely different.

For example, one of my brothers has a distracting habit of frowning, narrowing his eyes, and otherwise scrunching up his face whenever he is listening to new or complicated information he is trying to understand and assimilate. It looks for all the world as if he's very skeptical of what he's hearing and very negative on its validity. In fact, he hasn't rendered any judgment at all; it's just his way of concentrating on what is being said. Speakers who don't know this—and some who do—nevertheless tend to raise their voices, reiterate points, and otherwise sell harder to try to overcome what they perceive as his doubts. They usually end up doing themselves more harm than good.

To help you remember to watch your own body language in all situations, remember another three-word acronym: FAR—F-A-R:

- *Feel*
- *Adjust*
- *React*

Here's how it works:

F *Feel* the need to make a movement or gesture to reinforce or dramatize your words—or feel when you are doing something subconsciously.

A *Adjust* some part of your body to get it done or correct it.

R *React.* Examine how others *react* to your words and body movements together.

Like OLA, the elements of FAR are constantly changing. The reaction you see to your words and body language may require you to adjust again—for emphasis or for clarity. And the adjustment may cause you to feel different about what you are now conveying, forcing the cycle to begin all over again.

Although awkward at first, soon you will meld the observations/movements into your thinking. All it takes is practice.

PRACTICING WHAT IS PREACHED

PRACTICING WHAT IS PREACHED

Now let's try something—one of our interactive practice sessions. We like to give readers situations where they can use the learning we have provided and their own ideas to practice something we have just discussed.

Wherever you may be reading this book—in a favorite chair at home, while using an exercise machine, or perhaps in an airplane on a business trip—we hope you will enjoy taking a moment to suspend your reading to engage in some individual role playing involving body language. If, however, you prefer to practice at a different time or in a different place, we recommend that you simply put your bookmark on this page and restart when it is more convenient for you.

You will note that in all the role-playing sessions in this book, we create a scene for you and ask you to provide the body language to convey a meaning that for one reason or another you want to emphasize or cannot verbalize; conversely, we may ask you to interpret the meaning of the body language we have described for you.

We see these practice sessions as much more than idle exercises. We think that they could be important to you at some point down the road. Why? Because sometimes body language is the *only* means of communicating, intentionally or unintentionally, with someone else:

- In a foreign country, where you do not know the language.
- In a dangerous situation, where talking may be forbidden by captors, felons, or other bad guys.
- When you need to indicate something to someone else at a great distance—across an expanse of water, between two hills in the countryside, or while speeding along a highway in a car.
- When an idea comes to you that you want to communicate immediately, but silence is demanded. For example, during a sermon, in a library, at a piano recital, in a tense moment of a movie—or when it is impossible to make yourself understood—as a train whistle shrieks, when a band is particularly loud, or when a public-address announcer drones on during a sports event.
- Or when an involuntary movement, gesture, or expression provides sudden insights. It happened in a high profile lawsuit when the judge told jurors that four days of discussions were to be fogotten and that their deliberations had to begin again because he had instructed one of the alternates to join the panel. A reporter noted that one juror "rolled her eyes" when she heard the announcement from the bench and another "looked to the ceiling, then covered her eyes," suggesting that the experience was exasperating, the issues difficult, and the panel still arguing over the appropriate decision to reach.

For all of these reasons, getting good at body language may prove vital to you at some point. We are also reminded of an essential truth about the occasional superiority of body language over the spoken word: "Even a fish does all right when it keeps its mouth closed."

The scene we set for you and the gestures, movements, or tone we ask you to practice may be hard for you at first. Or you may be unsure how others will interpret what you have done. From time to time, we hope you can pretend to be a dance star, someone who has to rehearse before a mirror to determine if the muscles employed, the posture adopted, the gestures used, and the movements made are giving the exact look and meaning desired.

Enough introduction. Here's how the practice sessions will work. We will set a scene and then invite you into the action with instructions on the type of movement wanted or posture to adopt.

The Parking Lot—I

OK. You have probably been involved in this situation almost as many times as you have watched that scene from the detective story at the beginning of the book:

> *You are in your car in a parking lot moving steadily down a lane toward an exit when you see a sizable sport-utility vehicle (SUV) slowly approaching you from the opposite end of the lane. You also hear the engine of one of the parked cars start and then see a set of backup lights come on. The driver coming toward you also notices the same thing, slows markedly, then raises his hand just about to eye level with his palm facing him, flaps all of his fingers toward himself in two quick motions, then points his forefinger toward the place where the car is backing out before pumping his arm and hand twice across his chest.*

To make sure you're following our descriptions and can visualize the gestures, let's repeat them in square dance style. As you read the body language, we want you to try to duplicate the gesture described. Here we go:

> The driver coming toward you also hears the engine start and simultaneously notices a set of backup lights come on.

- He raises his hand just about to eye level...
  [DID YOU RAISE YOUR HAND TO THE SIDE OF YOUR FACE?]
- with his palm facing him...
  [DID YOU TURN YOUR FINGERS SO THAT YOU CAN SEE YOUR PALM?]
- flaps all his fingers toward him in two quick motions...
  [DID YOU BEND YOUR FINGERS AT THE KNUCKLES ON YOUR HAND IN UNISON IN TWO DELIBERATIVE "COME HERE" GESTURES?]
- then immediately points his forefinger toward the space and pumps his arm and hand twice across his chest.
  [DID YOU PUT YOUR HAND INTO A POINTING MOTION TO THE LEFT AND MOVE IT BACK AND FORTH TWICE?]

Fine. You got it. Now, describe to a mythical passenger in your car exactly what the other driver is indicating by this particular body language.

We imagine you had no problem figuring out that the other driver had spotted the space coming open and was indicating that he wanted you to come forward to go past him so that he could pull behind you into the soon-to-be-empty spot.

Now we'd like you to respond with your own body language. We'd like you to acknowledge to the other driver that you understood his gestures and are happy to comply with his request.

Did you ring your thumb and forefinger into a circle to indicate "OK," and then waggle your hand forward and back in a quick motion to signal your agreement?

Or, if the driver exiting the space has not yet completed his maneuvering, perhaps you moved your head up and down but held up your index finger. This would suggest to the driver of the SUV that you understood his request but that you are also asking him to wait a moment to allow you to comply.

All of these are simple gestures. They have a lot of meaning to anyone growing up in a Western culture.

Take a moment here to consider how simple and expressive body language can be. While it clearly doesn't have all the nuances of spoken language, it, too, can still have its share of subtlety. Take the hand. What would have been the meaning of the SUV driver's gesture had he not just flapped his fingers in a gentle curling fashion but had instead held his fingers rigid and vigorously moved his whole forearm back and forth from the elbow? Try it. Curl your fingers in an unhurried come hither gesture; then switch to a vigorous full arm movement.

Get the point? The first gesture is a *request;* the second is a *command.* The first is a sign of politeness; the second may indicate a greater element of urgency or even hostility. Of course, if the second gesture is made by a military policeman directing traffic—rather than by another driver—you could assume that the individual isn't being impatient so much as trying to be absolutely precise about what he wants to convey with his movements.

That brings us to the first rule of understanding body language. It must always be read in context—the context of the words that may accompany a movement as well as the situation in which the movement takes place.

Consider the use of the fingers in the hand movements that have been described. No need to tell anyone in the West that had the driver chosen to use his middle finger in a gesture, he would be conveying a ton of different meaning.

By the same token, the responding driver could have held up *his* index finger in a relaxed position, nail hidden, with his other fingers neatly folded down to indicate "wait a moment." Of course, had he used *his* middle finger to respond, or had he held his index finger up with the nail showing, it may have been misinterpreted by the SUV driver as a menacing gesture meaning: "I will not. No way. Forget it!"

Pause here a moment to consider these two gestures—the-come-forward-I-want-to-go-into-the-space gesture; and the response: I-understand-what-you-want-but-I-have-to-wait-a-moment. To help you master body language a little better, we would like you to show how these two gestures can be used to express different moods.

The Parking Lot—II

Now *you* are in the SUV and the parking garage is next to a movie house.

> *The film you want to see will be starting in five minutes. You know you have to purchase the tickets, buy the popcorn, go to the toilet, and get to your seats. How would you signal politely to the other driver to come forward to let you into the emptying space, but please do so with dispatch?*

Take a few moments to consider how you would handle the body language for this situation.

What did you think you might do? Had it been us, our sense of urgency would have been indicated by the speed of the gestures. The fingers would have been moving at twice the speed as before and we would have repeated the movement three times instead of once when the driver was under no pressure; the same for the forefinger thrusting across the chest to indicate where we wanted to go. The more vigorously we pointed, the greater we hoped we would be conveying the intensity of our request.

Now pretend you are the driver of the car waiting for the other car to back out of the space. You have seen the other driver's hand signals and you have indicated that you will comply in just a moment.

But in this scenario the SUV driver seems to be impatient. He leans on his horn for an extra long blast, then repeats his gesture with broad movements in slow motion as if you were mentally retarded. You don't want to get into a signaling argument with this arrogant snot, but you want to repeat that he has to wait a second because the other car is now blocking your way. OK, now repeat the gesture of understanding, but ask for patience.

If it had been us, we might have slowly waggled our forefinger side to side in a negative signal to suggest that we couldn't move at that moment and then instantly point several times toward the situation causing us the problem. We might also have held our whole palm up with a double patting motion—as if we were giving two deliberate high-five moves in succession— to suggest that the driver of the SUV simply had to wait for a moment before we would be capable of complying with his request.

UNDERSTANDING BODY LANGUAGE

UNDERSTANDING BODY LANGUAGE

The extraordinary power of nonverbal personal communication has been recognized in a number of academic studies. One of these found that *appearance*—what someone is wearing, how they present themselves—determines first impressions in fully 60 percent of the cases. The same study shows that only 7 percent of first impressions are based on what people actually *say* in a conversation—just 7 percent!!

Surprised? We were, given our faith in the power of *words*. But now that the findings have been confirmed in other research, we became believers. For example, researchers found that 55 percent of the subjects reacted to the *gestures* and *movements* they saw, not to the words they heard. In this study, the exact same words were used with the same voice cues but were accompanied with different physical movements, facial expressions, and hand gestures. In short, people responded to *how* a person said something, not *what* that person actually said.

Think about this before your next business or social conversation: The evidence seems pretty clear that the *gestures* you use, the *enthusiasm* you demonstrate, the *posture* you exhibit—in short, the *body language* you employ—do more to convince listeners of what it is you want to convey than all the words flowing from your lips.

As we have already seen, body language is not difficult and it is not rooted in some dictionary. Equally important, it gives those who "read" and "write" body language a wide range of choices. But also remember that *written or spoken* language is not necessarily unambiguous or always accurate in conveying meaning, either. Think about these examples:

- A message that recently raced around the world via EMail sounded like a college commencement speech that easily could have been written by author Kurt Vonnegut. It contained a lot of very amusing pieces of wisdom:

  * "Dance, even if you have nowhere to do it but your living room."
  * "Be kind to your knees. You'll miss them when they're gone."
  * "Keep your old love letters. Throw away your old bank statements."

  But it turns out Mr. Vonnegut neither delivered the piece nor wrote it. Rather, these lines first appeared as a column in a Boston newspaper. It was as if one person passed the column to another with a comment to the effect that "it *sounds* like something Kurt Vonnegut might have written." Several relays later, the "sounds like something" got lost and an Internet legend was born.

- In the book *Beyond Justice,* author F. Anthony Macklin relates the following story that shows that some things work better in *oral* English than in the written form. One of the characters in the book relates the following riddle:

  What do you get when you cross Lassie with a watermelon?

The answer is...

Melancholy.

That's worth a groan when *hearing* the joke for the first time but totally confusing when the spelling differences in the two key words are presented in a written version.

Another author, Tom Wolfe, uses body language extensively to convey the attitudes of his characters. Here are three examples from his novel *A Man In Full*:

- *Arthur Lomprey turned and looked at her, and his smile spread so far she could have counted his teeth. But his eyes were pure panic. They contracted into little frozen balls. "May Day!" they said. "Code Blue! I've seen this woman somewhere before, but who in the name of God is she?"*
- *Roger eyed him warily—but Partridge broke into a grin and said heartily: 'Heyyyyy, Roger! How's our in-house celebrity this morning?' It was the grin, more than what he said, that did it, and Roger relaxed.*
- *"He slapped the tops of his knees in the way that says 'That wraps it up. It's time to go,' then he stood up, with a feeble lurch..."*

If body language can add meaning to spoken or written words, so they can also detract from the effect of other forms of expression. We all know the haunting tones of *Taps* and the emotional impact it evokes. We were amazed to learn recently that the tones have been set to words in three verses. Although very well done, they seem to add nothing to the music. Judge for yourself. The first and third stanzas are presented here as a sample of our point:

I

Day is done
Gone the sun
From the lakes
From the hills

From the sky
All is well
Safely rest
God is nigh.

III

Thanks and praise
For our days
Neath the sun
Neath the stars

Neath the sky
As we go
This we know
God is nigh.

Let's turn now to other aspects of body language that also impact the messages people receive from you.

Clothing, for example, is often said to make the man. The meaning of this saying, of course, is that the way someone dresses conveys details about attitudes and philosophy. But like so much else in body language, you need to put the clothing into an appropriate context before interpreting its meaning. For example, the expected dress at the Academy Awards ceremony is black tie for men, formal gowns for women. If an actor arrives at the ceremony in a black suit with satin lapels but is wearing a white wing-collared shirt and checkered four-in-hand tie, is he pioneering a style or a rebel against convention? Of course, someone else might ask, Is he under contract to a clothing designer or was some of his luggage misplaced by an airline?

Take the Super Bowl. Half the United States, or so some estimate, go somewhere to watch the game on television. It has become one of America's annual cultural rituals. We would guess that of the 100 million men who attended a Super Bowl party this past January, not *one* wore a tie to the event intentionally; if these same millions were invited to visit the president in the Oval Office, however, we would guess that all but a bare handful would almost certainly wear a tie for the occasion. How do we learn these conventions?

By observation, rather than by overt teaching or direct questioning. As a result, when someone wears clothing outside of what the vast majority perceive as the norms of dress in the context of the situation in which he or she will appear, then we notice the difference. When we do, we need to pay close attention because it is likely that some kind of extra message is being communicated by nonverbal means.

Interpreting the message is both intriguing and often difficult. Remember, a guy on his way to jail with a rap sheet as long as the hood of a race car may be wearing a single earring. A similar solitary earring may also be seen on basketball great Michael Jordan and *60 Minutes* reporter Ed Bradley. In short, the earring by itself will suggest some things about the individual wearing it, but it won't be a definitive telltale in describing his personality.

As a result, people have to be careful about drawing hard and fast conclusions from the body language they observe. It is much better to formulate a theory about the meaning of the clothing or accessory. Then see if subsequent actions, known facts, and any words spoken fit the body language or the clothing exhibited.

In short, be cautious! But in a phrase, don't be afraid of combining all the information being conveyed to you into a coherent story.

A Little Background

As noted in the introduction, our interest in the whole topic of body language started with our study of word of mouth advertising more than 10 years ago. At the time, we were working for a client of our public policy consulting firm involved in tourism. We argued that most people choose a travel destination based on what their friends and associates tell them rather than on some paid advertisement they see in a newspaper or some brochure they receive in the mail. Intrigued, the client asked us to write a paper on the topic. While we found a lot of anecdotal evidence and research studies supporting the *importance* of word of mouth advertising, we could find no detailed case studies discussing successfully employed word of mouth programs.

We soon learned that most advertising agencies charge a percentage of the cost of an advertisement placement for their services rather than a flat fee. Designed word of mouth programs cost almost nothing to create or operate. As a result, most ad agencies choose to adopt what we call a tooth fairy attitude toward word of mouth advertising. If the gossip gods smile on a product, service, place, or event, favorable word of mouth comments are likely to result, and that's good. If the gossip gods are not inclined to favor an item, nothing more can be done to stimulate word of mouth comments. In other words, ad agencies in our view don't worry much about word of mouth advertising because they can't figure out how to get paid for it.

Coming out of a political background—where all policy ideas have to be molded and shaped until they are understood and accepted by the public—we found this made no sense. So we began to assemble a collection of ideas on how word of mouth comments might be stimulated. We were looking for ways to help businesses make their customers into part of their sales force. We think that by now we have succeeded. Many of our ideas are recorded in four different books on the topic of word of mouth advertising: *Talk Is Cheap, How to Generate Word of Mouth Advertising, Don't Take Our Word For It!,* and *Let Your Fingers Do the Talking.*

If interest in the 22 different foreign language versions of these books is any indication, word of mouth is growing as a legitimate form of market promotion around the world, much as the Internet has become an effective new player in retailing. As we noted in the Introduction, there is a reason for this. It stems from the public's growing doubts about the truthfulness of traditional forms of promotion. Most of us know instinctively that media advertising is inherently dishonest. Sponsors seldom reveal the whole truth about their products or services, seldom compare themselves to competitors, and are generally reluctant to waste time or space telling us when a product is not very effective or shouldn't even be used by some people. When did you last see an ad, for instance, showing passengers having a *lousy* time on board a cruise ship or visitors *losing* money in a Las Vegas casino?

The same is true for another form of promotion: public relations. We have become so familiar with its self-serving nature that we use the word "spin" to describe how any set of facts is turned to reveal its most favorable side. Finally, product presentations have become just another questionable promotional device. If an oversized container is not masking a shrinking supply, then it is picturing something that few can hope to obtain or replicate in real life or it is proclaiming something that is most likely an exaggeration of reality.

What's left in the realm of promotion is word of mouth advertising. *Real* word of mouth advertising is effective because friends, relatives, and associates talk to each other about products or services one knows or has had some experience with. By and large, friends and relatives have no reason to embellish the truth and no conflict of interest to taint their viewpoints; what they say can be safely taken as an honest expression of their opinion about a product or service. That's why it is so well trusted; that's why word of mouth is so effective.

Some have come to value word of mouth so highly that they consider it almost immoral to give out false or exaggerated information—to anyone. Listen to what an American entrepreneur said to the media about what he tells friends interested in joining him in doing business in Vietnam: "I [do] not feel I [can], in good faith, encourage others to invest their money in a country as complicated and risky as [this one.]"

There is one other basic aspect of word of mouth commentary worth emphasizing. Just because some people have something favorable to say about a product or service does not necessarily mean they will, in fact, say it. In short, word of mouth is not automatic; even close relations and good friends do not generally speak on their own about the power of the staple gun they use or the quality of the furniture wax they buy. As a result, we have come to believe that every business needs to have at least one program in place to encourage their current customers speak about their products and services to others. These programs end up as not only the cheapest form of promotion a business can develop but also among the most effective they can employ.

We have also come to believe that there is a relationship between a successful word of mouth program and those adept at conversation. People who are comfortable and enjoy talking to others tend to be more fluent and more convincing at transferring interest in a product or service to someone else. Our book *Talk Is Easy—How to Make Every Conversation Pay Off* is filled with ideas and hints that help make any conversation less taxing and more rewarding.

But as has been pointed out above, conversation turns out to be much more than just the *words* someone speaks. It has a great deal to do with the gestures, movements, and voice tones one adopts; people, it seems, pay more attention to what they *see* than to what they *hear*; they gain a major part of their impressions of a product, service, or event by what they observe in the person providing the information rather than by what that person actually says about an item.

Hence we knew that if we were really going to help people use word of mouth advertising, then we had to help them understand the role that body language can play in conveying facts and feelings. It is an important part of how we communicate and what others learn from us.

PRACTICING AGAIN

PRACTICING AGAIN

Let's conduct another practice session at this point. To demonstrate the impact of voice cues along with movement and posture, we are going to ask you to say the same simple sentence out loud in various settings. The sentence is: "I am really looking forward to this." OK. Say the sentence out loud a few times to get comfortable with the words: "I am really looking forward to this."—"I am really looking forward to this."—"I am really looking forward to this."

Now say the same sentence a couple of times as if you were sitting in a lawyer's office before being read the last will and testament of a long lost uncle.

We bet your voice was up, full of energy, with a lot of emphasis on the word "really." When we tried it with the mythical circumstances in mind, this is how it sounded to us:

"I am...REALLY...looking forward to *THIS*!"

OK, now we want you to try the very same sentence as if you were a law student facing your second try at the bar examination.

We assume you fairly spat those words out with just enough sarcasm in your voice to make sure that *no one* missed the point that you really *weren't* very pleased to be in the same position you were just six months before with the possibility that you may have to explain to friends and relatives yet another failure when the results of this exam are finally published.

Now let's try adding some additional meaning to the sentence

"I am really looking forward to this"

through body language. But we want you to do this without employing any gestures or voice cues. The only tool you have is your *physical posture.*

Pretend your boss has called you into her office to tell you the details of the raise the personnel committee has approved for you. Take a moment to arrange yourself in that straight-backed chair at the side of her desk. If, as you read this, you are not in a position to actually adopt this posture, just picture in your mind exactly how you think you would be sitting at this instance…

Are your shoulders squared, your backbone ramrod straight? Are you on the edge of the chair with your body turned to face the boss directly? Good. You are showing the kind of body language that conveys alertness, interest, and attentiveness.

But what if, instead of a meeting with your boss to learn about your raise, you are in a large conference room with your colleagues and you haven't had a chance to read the thick background paper that will be discussed. You certainly intended to read it last night, but you fell asleep before you could get past page 10. In this case, do you pick out a seat right across from the individual chairing the meeting or do you search for a place out of his direct line of sight?

We think you would try to find a seat in the corner on the perfectly understandable theory that out-of- sight means out-of-mind.

OK. The chairman comes in, sits down, states the issues on which he is anxious to hear staff views, and begins to look around for the first person to call upon. Describe the kind of posture you might adopt in your chair at this instant.

Did you shrink a little in your seat to create a smaller target for the chairman to see? Did you adopt a facial expression of boredom, as if the issues weren't important or you had more important things to do? Did you lower your head, pretending to be looking for the right quotation or the right point but suggesting that you are not quite ready to respond should the chairman decide to call on you? All are good body language strategies that some bureaucrats learn to perfection.

But what if you came to the meeting having read the paper and with definite ideas on the issues posed by the chairman? You are eager to speak and let the others know how you feel. Where are you sitting now? How is your posture? Where are your eyes focused when the chairman comes in?

Let's take a moment now to interpret the kind of body language you see every day:

- You are watching the final moments of a National Basketball Association game on a television set above the bar in a restaurant. Your team is behind but has the ball with just seconds left. It is passed to the best shooter on the team, who immediately goes up for his jump shot. At that instant, a waiter drops a tray of dishes. You automatically look to see the aftermath of the accident. When you look back to the television, the camera is focused on the shooter walking toward the sideline. You don't need the announcer to tell you that the shot didn't go down and the game is lost; the slump in his shoulders and the limp position of his arms are all that needs to be said.

- You are in the waiting room at a doctor's office. You look up briefly from your magazine to see an older woman furiously rubbing her hand over her left arm while staring off into space. It doesn't take much imagination to realize that she is feeling cold as she anxiously waits to find out something the doctor obviously knows—the results of some medical test, the type of therapy she will have to endure, and so on.

- In a game of poker, you see a young player across from you absently brushing the tip of his forefinger across his eyebrow while clutching his cards tightly in his other hand. What does this mean in terms of the cards he is holding? To an experienced player, this is called a "tell." It is the kind of indicator that says he is quizzical, wondering whether his good hand is good enough. He is hoping to win without a struggle with the other players. His body language is suggesting that he might be vulnerable to some aggressive bets and raises if any of his opponents have a strong hand.

- As you are driving home you decide to take the freeway instead of surface streets. As you start gaining speed on the on-ramp you see a highway patrolman waiting in his car. You atomatically take your foot off of the accelerator, but then notice him motioning with his right hand, pulling it diagonally down across his chest. No words spoken, but no doubt that he is telling you to fasten your seat belt harness. You move to comply in the next heartbeat, lest he decide you need a stronger lesson in driving safety.

- You are sitting behind a couple at a concert. The guy is tall, but he won't sit still. He keeps shifting his body in his seat, first turning his left side into

> the back of the chair, then going 180° the other way to press his right side against the back. What is happening here? Is he expressing boredom or just trying to stay awake? Maybe he has a bad back. In this case, as we have noted before, without other clues or other knowledge the body language alone may not be enough to determine his mental state.

What does each of these cases suggest to you? That you have been producing and reacting to body language a lot more than you might have realized. Our effort here is to refine the skills you already have and to get you to use body language to your own advantage whenever selling a product, a service, or an idea through word of mouth commentary.

POP QUIZ

POP QUIZ

George Stephanopoulos was one of President Bill Clinton's closest advisers during Clinton's first election campaign and his first term of office. He observed the president and Mrs. Clinton in dozens of different situations.

He described their particular body language in his book *All Too Human—A Political Education.* Let's have a little fun at this point. We'd like you to take the following multiple-choice quiz to see how well you do at explaining what you think was on the mind of either the president or Mrs. Clinton from the body language described by Stephanopoulos in his book:

- Stephanopoulos writes that *"Bill Clinton had the gait of a man used to being obeyed, admired, courted, and loved."*

  You would therefore expect the pace and movement in the president's walk to involve:

  A. Short steps at a slow speed.

  B. Medium-length strides at a purposeful speed.

  C. Long deliberate steps as if he were measuring distances.

  D. Short tippy-toe steps as if to keep his feet out of puddles in the street.

We are sure you picked "B'—medium-length strides at a purposeful speed. In other words, President Clinton walks with a clear goal in mind, never seeming to hesitate or give a hint of being unsure of the direction he wants to move. We think that indeed describes the "gait of a man used to being obeyed, admired, courted, and loved."

Here is the second question.

- Stephanopoulos describes Hillary Rodham Clinton in this way: *"The fear in [her] face was masked a bit by the heavy makeup she wore for the cameras, but I had seen it before. The tight smile, the fixed gaze, the hands folded firmly in her lap..."*

  This kind of body language describes:

  A. Someone who has eaten too much and fears what the scale will reveal the next morning.

  B. Someone who is worried about the nature of the questions she will be asked and how she will answer them.

  C. Someone who is bracing herself for bad news.

  D. Someone who hasn't slept enough and is trying to take attention away from the bags under her eyes.

The answer is "B" again. Stephanopoulos said he saw the body language whenever Mrs. Clinton was anticipating having to answer difficult questions about what she considered to be her family's private affairs.

OK. The third question.

- Stephanopoulos writes: *"[One of Clinton's moods] was the silent scream. No yelling, no finger in your face, nothing. Just silence. I would walk into the office, and he wouldn't look up; the slightly formal "Hello, George" would sound more like an irritating obligation than a greeting."*

  When exhibiting this behavior, would you think the president was:

  A. Mad about something that had occurred?

  B. Distracted by something that should not have occurred?

  C. Irritated by something about to occur?

  D. Any or all of the above?

Here the answer is "D." Stephanopoulos reports that they never knew when the president would arrive in the Oval Office with a mad on, but not knowing what caused it or how to fix it was one of the most difficult issues for the personal staff to deal with.

Final question in our little pop quiz.

- Stephanopoulos reports the following. *"[When members of Congress told Clinton that] an unequivocal statement of presidential support on affirmative action was essential, Clinton took notes, bit his lip, and nodded his head in vigorous agreement."*

  According to Stephanopoulos, did this presidential body language:

  A. Indicate the president agreed on providing an unequivocal statement of support?

  B. Suggest merely that the president agreed with the need for a statement without necessarily agreeing to issue such a statement?

  C. Show that the president was concerned about how to handle the issue without approving any particular strategy?

  D. Demonstrate that the president was bored with the discussion. By biting his lip he held back saying what he knew he shouldn't and by taking notes he was trying to occupy himself to stop from falling asleep?

Here the actual answer was "C." The president wanted to show *concern,* not *approval.* But Stepanopolus noted that the members of Congress were "thrilled, convinced they had a promise from the president" to support affirmative action. In this actual situation, the president protested: "I didn't say that." But his chief of staff told him that his *body language* did not leave any "door [still] open."

How did you do on our little quiz? Did you ace it? We figure that if you got at least two of the correct answers, you are well on your way to having a strong understanding of body language.

BUSINESS SITUATIONS

BUSINESS SITUATIONS

Now it's time to put some of this learning about body language into some specific business situations. Here, we will describe some body language; your job is to describe what you think it may mean.

- *You are a salesperson who finally obtained a long-sought- after appointment with the company CEO. Three minutes after you begin your presentation, your audience of one begins to drum his fingers—pinky to index finger—rapidly and repeatedly on the arm of his high- backed chair.*

  What do you think this means and what do you do with your knowledge?

Drumming the fingers in this way is a clear signal of impatience or boredom. The CEO is signaling you to get to the heart of the presentation, to stop all the preliminary chatter, and background explanations. He either wants you to get to the bottom line—how will what you are selling him help his company—or wants to guide your presentation by telling you something about his needs or his company's procedures.

As a result of seeing the body language, you need to ask him a question—"Is this clear?" "Should I know something more about your thinking?"—to determine the direction in which to proceed.

If his answer is abrupt or perfunctory, he is clearly not in a mood to tell you more than he thinks you absolutely need to know. You should go immediately to the key points of how your product or service will help him. If, however, his answer is a long and expansive response, you need to fit the remainder of your presentation within the parameters he has just set.

Another situation.

- *You are interviewing for a new position in a rapidly expanding company. You want the job and think that you have thus far made a good impression. But as you continue talking, you notice that the personnel manager has converted his pencil into a drumstick. With the eraser end of the pencil between his thumb and forefinger, he absently begins to bounce its tip on the desktop.*

  What should you do?

While this behavior generally tends to suggest that the person wishes to be doing something different or to be somewhere else, it is usually a solitary act or may even be exhibited only when hearing some kind of recorded music. To suddenly exhibit this type of body language with a complete stanger in a conversational setting suggests she isn't paying attention to what is going on around her.

The best way to deal with an unusual situation is to confront it head on. In this case you need to inquire directly and politely about the behavior—*May I ask if there is a reason you are playing the* Star-Spangled Banner *with such precision?* or you can deal with it humorously—*If you are trying to signal me in Morse Code with your pencil, I am afraid that I missed a crucial vowel or two along the way.*

Just as you sometimes have to ask someone to repeat a word or define a meaning, here is a perfect example of when you need to ask directly for a definition of the body language you are observing.

Another example:

- *You can't hear the conversation across the room, but you can certainly see everything going on. You observe two ladies and a man in animated conversation. The man is describing something. Suddenly, one of the women throws both of her hands across her mouth as her eyes go wide open.*

  How do you read the lady's body language?

While you certainly don't know the specifics of what the man said, the wide eyes is a clear signal of having just heard something astonishing. The sudden covering of the mouth is usually a sign that the listener is repressing what he or she really feels like saying in reaction at that instant. It is the body's demand to remain quiet, to say nothing, and maintain a neutral position in face of the information she has just acquired.

If the same conversation resulted in one of the ladies' slapping her own face lightly with one or even both hands, it would be a sign of even greater shock or amazement at what had just been said. It would not be a sign that the lady wanted to repress her reaction.

If instead of the hands flying to the cheeks, they were instead used to cover the eyes, it is a sign of embarrassment. The individual hearing whatever is being said literally doesn't want to *look* further at the situation being described.

OK. A final element of body language in a business situation:

- *You are new to a company and joining a meeting for the first time. You notice that every time the leader gives the floor to one of your new colleagues, she turns to look at you as if she is seeking your approval. She outranks you by several steps, you are not yet fully comfortable with all of the material being discussed, and you are not sure how best to respond to the attention she is giving you.*

  How do you deal with this situation?

Remember OLA—*Oberve, Link, Analyze*. You need to be sure you have thought through all the possible implications before doing anything.

So begin to *Observe*: Is this staring consistent? Has she done it *each* time she has called on a different person? Your memory says yes and after she asks someone else a question, her look in your direction confirms it.

Now *Link* the behavior—is there something that makes her think that you are someone else? Is there anything around you that is giving off wrong signals? Are you wearing something or doing something that might give her reason for her behavior? Could this be personal and not related to the business situation?

Finally *Analyze* your immediate situation...what are your choices to respond to her gaze? You could adopt a neutral facial expression that indicates neither approval nor disapproval of whatever she is doing. You could avoid her gaze by being sure to look away—at your papers, out the window, in a briefcase—the next time she calls on someone different. Or you could be very positive and return her smile and nod approvingly whenever she looks your way.

At that moment, you hear the speaker thank an individual for her presentation and you know that the leader will soon be calling on the next person. How are you going to handle her gaze this next time?

There is, of course, no *right* answer here, only YOUR answer. Had it been us, given all the circumstances described, we think we would have taken the third choice and been enthusiastic and approving. We figured that to be neutral might send signals that could be misinterpreted and to try to avoid eye contact might suggest that you are unwilling to fully participate on your new team. Being enthusiastic and approving, of course, does not mean that you cannot discreetly enquire after the meeting if this kind of behavior is usual or whether it carries some hidden meaning.

Two more stories about the impact of body language and how revealing it can be in conveying information: Some years ago we noted in our book *From Trash to Treasure* how body language separates the buyers from the lookers at swap meets. Here is how we described these differences in body language:

> *Buyers...tend to inspect items closely—they pick them up, turn them over, talk about them, and generally study every facet of an object to determine condition, size, quality, strength, and value. Lookers, on the other hand, tend to point to items or bend over them. They don't talk much. If they pick something up, they finger it casually and generally put it down quickly.*
>
> *Buyers usually plant their feet in front of a dealer's display, generally standing still when considering a purchase. Lookers tend to keep their bodies moving, sometimes strolling, sometimes shuffling sideways, but always moving.*

We no longer work the swap meets, but we have been spending a lot of time at book shows lately. The body language we observe in the aisles is exactly the same. If they are strolling with their heads turned sideways at a 45° angle, they are merely passing by; if they stop and look squarely into a booth to study the titles, they are serious potential buyers. Last year at the huge Frankfurt

Book Fair we had another example of body language telling us more than the words being spoken.

An author was showing us the Italian version of a guide book she had written. It depicted all the places in Rome that were to have significance in the celebration of the millennium in the year 2000. It was meticulously detailed in its descriptions and beautifully illustrated with maps, diagrams, and color photographs. She thought we would be likely candidates to translate the book into English for sale in the United States.

We had another idea and told her about our own experience with a map overlay book we had published on the changing geographic face of the former Soviet Union. We thought it would be a winner among schools and universities interested in having their students understand how the economic forces, ethnic groups, and transportation systems of a previously unified superpower were divided among 15 independent countries. It didn't turn out to be so. We didn't sell many copies of our atlas in the United States, but we did sell a pleasing number to tourists through the major hotels in the big Russian cities.

So we told this Italian author that instead of looking for an American publisher, she should be seeking an *Italian* publisher willing to publish an English-language version for tourists going to Italy. I started to explain how expensive I thought it would be to find only those Americans interested in sites in Rome of significance during the millennium celebrations. Instead of listening, the author began to pack her papers and close the sample book. Recognizing this body language as an indication that she wanted to escape the impact of my words, I stopped the speech. So intent was she at getting away that she didn't even even realize I was no longer talking to her.

While some body language is involuntary, a lot of it can be controlled to give off the right signals to get the best possible response from your listeners. It is identical to the problem of knowing the right questions to ask to get the kind of information you want.

Here is an example: You know how you get calls around dinner time from some overly cheerful person who greets you by name and asks how you are? It is the dreaded telemarketer with some pitch for a newspaper subscription, a charitable donation, or a new long-distance telephone service. Your first reaction is to slam the phone down, and your second reaction is to figure out how to escape having to hear more or how to create the excuse to get out of the conversation.

Recently, the time was right and the phone rang. I picked it up. "Hello, Mr. Mayer?" I hear after a slight hesitation. At this point you need to know that my wife has retained the name of her former husband for the sake of her kids. As soon as I hear someone expecting to speak with "Mrs." Mayer and having to switch gears to talk with someone they assume is "Mr." Mayer, I go into one of my escape modes.

"No, he's dead" is one of my favorite end-the-conversation gambits when I am in a hurry. (The John Mayer in question died in a plane accident some 20 years ago.) It is the kind of response that leaves callers befuddled as to what to say. I used it on that recent call. As I am hanging up the phone I hear the caller gulp and say she was very sorry. Fine.Two minutes later, though, the phone rings again. I pick it up and the first words I hear are "This is Fisk-It Plumbing Service. Is Miguel there yet?" Same voice, same intonation.

It is clearly the same caller, but this time she has asked the right question to get the kind of response that she wants.

So it is with body language. If you give off the right signals with your movements, gestures, and expressions, you will get the reaction you want from your listeners—no matter the precision of your words.

NOT TOO SUBTLE, PLEASE

NOT TOO SUBTLE, PLEASE

The importance of body language occurred to me the other Sunday. I was hitting tennis balls in the park against a backboard. Behind me in the parking lot a cluster of guys was still gathering their soccer equipment from the back of a van and another group off to the right was just starting a two-on-two basketball game.

The quiet still of the early morning was suddenly broken by the wail of an emergency siren. All the people within my vision stopped what they were doing and automatically turned toward the sound. For some reason, each of us wants to determine the source of such sounds. As the vehicle rounded a corner, we all saw that it was a fire engine, but that fact alone did not give us any more information about the main question: The nature of the problem it was responding to. It didn't matter. All of us froze like the actors in the famous horse racing scene in "My Fair Lady." We were riveted in place, slowly turning our heads to follow the progress of the truck as it roared down the boulevard.

I was the farthest away from the street, so I could see the other guys at the back of the van and on the basketball court. We were all watching intently. It suggested to me that the fire truck was an apt metaphor for the importance of body language. No words need be spoken so long as a movement is bold enough to draw attention and to spark interpretation. It made me think that if you want your body language to mean something, you need to make your gestures large and your movements deliberate, and you may want to accompany some changes in posture with a unique sound.

Bill Walton made the same point during the telecast of a professional basketball game one week. The Miami Heat were playing the New York Knicks. Alonzo Mourning, one of the top players for the Heat, was bumped by an opposing New York Knicks player some distance from the basket. Mourning made a chili stew of the contact, bouncing back as if he had hit a freeway retaining wall at 60 mph, all the while flailing his arms in an exaggerated attempt to regain his balance. Instantly, a whistle sounded and a foul was called. Walton scoffed. He said that the referee never paid much attention to the original contact but could hardly ignore the body language before a vociferous home crowd.

Same with the bigger-than-life cartoon characters at theme parks and team mascots at athletic events. Watch how good they are at conveying emotions of joy and sadness, stirring up a crowd, making people laugh, all without the benefit of any sound or facial expressions. The only thing available to them is greatly exaggerated body movements. It's actually fairly impressive.

The important point to remember whenever using body language to reinforce words or to express an idea is don't be subtle. Let your gestures and movements be seen and let others react to them more than to your words.

One other point needs to be made about the subtlety of body language. Large movements can work both ways—for you if you are doing the expressing and against you if you are on the receiving end. Here is an example we have all experienced: We are pitching a new idea, product, or service to someone else and we see that person nodding vigorously. Most of us take the nodding for approval of what we are presenting—mostly because we desperately want to read the body language in this way. Few of us, unfortunately, perceive the nod as merely one of *understanding*. While the listener may be showing a positive response to our point, he may also be simply acknowledging the fact that he is *getting* it rather than the fact that he is *buying* it.

The point is that if you are not sure what some aspect of body language is intending to convey, ask for clarification. You can do that by asking directly if the individual understands and accepts what is being said. By the same token, the same information can be sought indirectly by asking for some form of agreement or willingness to take a subsequent step.

Asking for what you want may not get you the answer you hope for, but it certainly limits the danger of relying on the ambiguity inherent in some types of communication.

AUTOMATIC BODY LANGUAGE

AUTOMATIC BODY LANGUAGE

Now let's look at one of the most important aspects of body language—reading the *involuntary* gestures and movements of others. These gestures and movements can tell you what the other person is *really* thinking or feeling about a topic or at a particular time. We first raised the subject when we asking you to interpret finger drumming and pencil tapping in an interview situation and when we told you the story of the guide book author at a book show.

We've all seen this type of body language...a sudden turn, a subconscious movement, a twitch of the facial muscles. Here are just some that we, ourselves, have observed:

- When people cross their arms across their chest, it is generally interpreted as a protective move—people are guarding against some kind of assault from an idea, a question, a position, or an invasion of their psychological territory. They have made their arms into a barrier; penetration becomes more difficult.
- You have seen it. People bring the fingertips of both of their hands together to form a church steeple. In fact, psychologists refer to this gesture as "steepling." It is usually associated with people who are hoping that their comments will be accepted and believed by the listener. Salespeople

tend to use the gesture a lot; when you see it, listen carefully to make sure you understand all the details of the presentation.

- "I don't know who did it, but don't blame me for leaving the hall light on." Brave, bold statements like these, accompanied by some unconscious move like rubbing a hand across the brow (figuratively wiping the sweat away), usually indicates someone is really not sure of his statement despite the positive tone of voice used.
- Two people meet at the copying machine in an office. They exchange a few words about a sports event or a program on television. Then one asks the other when he might expect to hear about his project. As the subject is being broached, the listener starts to turn away and become engrossed in the buttons to push to get his copies made. The physical movement suggests that the listener is trying to escape, to get away from the topic—for any one of a dozen reasons such as he hadn't gotten around to looking at the issue or he hadn't sent the paperwork to the committee or he had received a preliminary indication that no approval would be granted that year. Whatever the reason, the body language indicates that he does not want to talk about this topic at this moment at this place within the geography of the office.

Besides involuntary body language, let's look now at *group* body language—the movements we all seem to use to subtly pass messages to others that we don't want to articulate in words. Here, we want to describe a situation and then pause for a moment so that you can think through why that body language is being used.

- *What happens typically when Americans get into an elevator already containing other passengers?*

They immediately face front, invariably focus their eyes on the floor indicator, and generally make no noise. It is group body language that recognizes that talking in close quarters would be intrusive of the privacy of others.

- *What happens when an American arrives at an ATM already in use by someone else?*

He or she waits patiently about two meters behind the machine to avoid even the appearance that the newcomer may be trying to see something displayed on the monitor. No one decided this distance, and no one painted a line on the sidewalk in front of banks; it was simply something that the culture determined for itself based on unwritten rules of the proper distance to allow for privacy.

- *What happens when two Americans are in conversation for the first time in several months in front of a supermarket?*

They separate themselves by an arm's length. If one tries to press closer—or is forced closer by someone passing behind—the other tends to back away. The next time you are in such a conversation, note that you are just about a meter from the other individual. When Americans are at an overcrowded cocktail party and the crush of people pushes individuals closer than is normally acceptable, note how uncomfortable everyone gets and watch their eyes dart around as they look for open space in the room or on a balcony to move to. Anglo Americans need that yard of separation to be comfortable. Anything closer and we feel we are in a zone usually reserved, and more appropriate, for intimate contact.

But watch two people have the same sort of conversation on the streets of Khartoum or Cairo, and you will see them standing to converse within a foot of each other. Although *we* may feel uncomfortable when others press this close, it is a matter of culture, not the delivery of a physical threat or sexual message that is involved.

What does this group body language mean? If you want to break through to people—literally if you want to stand out in a crowd—recognize the norms we all accept when we are in groups and then set about exceeding those boundaries.

We will guarantee you that when you do something that breaks the rules, people will notice, comment, and take action!

VOICE CUES

VOICE CUES

Now let's turn once again to other forms of nonverbal communication. Take voice cues. We call them the half-way house between words and physical movements. They are the tone, speed, pitch, vocabulary, and grammar used when talking. It is a form of body language that we probably use more often than any other.

Listen to how famous novelist John Grisham uses voice cues in his novel *The Testament.*

> *"There was a slight pause as Valdir changed [topics].*
>
> *"'We're having a small Christmas party in my home this afternoon. Just my family and a few friends. Would you like to join us?'*
>
> *"There was a stiffness to the invitation. Nate couldn't tell if Valdir was only trying to be polite, or if it was a matter of language and accent."*

Grisham's character refuses the invitation because the *tone of voice* in which the invitation was issued made it sound perfunctory.

Tom Wolfe, another great American novelist, also spends a lot of time describing voice cues as a signal of meaning in his book *A Man In Full.* In one discussion between an accountant nicknamed the Wiz and his boss, the conversation went this way:

"'—-it's not something I want to see happen—but what about [selling] the plantation?'

"Incredulous: 'Turpmtine?'

"'Well, I mean, only in the sense that here we have a non-core asset...not creating any particular synergies.' The Wiz's diction was beginning to degenerate into sheer technogeekspeak gibberish...out of fear. He knew he had blundered onto dangerous ground with his boss."

Think about it. Wolfe uses only one word—"incredulous"—to describe the tone of voice used in a one-word question—"Turpmtine?"(By the way, the spelling of "Turpmtine" is precisely how Wolfe uses it in his novel.) But that one word is enough for the reader to hear in his head the full fury behind the boss's unhappiness with his accountant's suggestion.

Here are some other quotes from Tom Wolfe's *A Man In Full*. Listen to how he describes his characters and their reactions to events through the voice cues he has them give:

- *"One more thing," he said. "Just remember: speak firmly but slowly and in a low voice, a normal voice. People take a loud, hurried voice to mean you're insecure."*
- *"'Charlie,' said Serena, 'I'm going to drive our car home [from the hospital]. I'll try to get there before you do...' There was nothing wrong with what she said, but he didn't like the tone. It was the tone of frustration and suppressed rage with which you address a hopeless invalid who insists on making inroads into your free time."*

Tone, speed, volume—all important indicators of the message beyond the words. They are both controllable and manageable. Some voice matters are not. Concert singers, for example, often demand scent-free areas backstage. Luciano Pavarotti's standard contracts with impresarios are said to call for "...no distinct smells anywhere near the artist." Promoters say that odors from fresh paint, furniture oils, and even some flowers can constrict the voices or adversely impact the sinuses.

Many individuals suffer from similar problems after being asleep for a while, often sounding gruff, thick, or even slow as they first come awake. All of us have suffered from laryngitis, colds, and coughs that impact the sound and rhythm of our voices.

As in all matters relative to body language, try to understand the context before irrevocably reacting to a body language incident.

WORKING WORD OF MOUTH

WORKING WORD OF MOUTH

Now to another theme. We mentioned at the outset of this book that we saw a connection between successful word of mouth advertising and effective body language. We believe *how* someone says something about a product or service counts a lot more than the words they might use to describe the same thing. In fact, Robin Dunbar, in his book *Grooming, Gossip, and the Evolution of Language,* suggests body language actually amounts to two-thirds of how we interpret the meaning of any message.

Because of this, we have often been asked in the seminars we conduct for business groups whether there are ways to get customers to use aspects of body language when telling someone else about a product or service.

Yes, we answer, and proceed to give a number of examples. Here are a few of them:

- The best teacher I ever had in any school I ever attended was a wonderful man named Ed Lindop. One day when we were studying the Italian Renaissance, he was determined that his world history students would never forget the exact definition of a "fresco painting." So he gave us a syncopated chant that I have always remembered, even though it has been more than 50 years since I first heard it.

Mr. Lindop told us that a fresco is just *"A WATER COLOR PAINTING ON A [WAIT ONE BEAT] DAMP PLASTER WALL."* We sang that little chant in unison so often that it became a part of our very being.

With the concept in mind, see if you can come up with a way to describe your own product, service, or business in a simple rhythmic way. We, ourselves, once developed a little poem for clients in travel-related businesses to give to their customers on luggage tags. The poem went like this:

BACKS STAY FINE—AND IN LINE—
WHEN YOU SAY EACH DAY:

Stretch a bit,
if you sit.
Never twist,
as you lift.
Bend the knees—
gently, please.

Remember Johnny Cochran's famous use of rhyme in his jury summation during the O.J. Simpson trial. His rap were variations on: "If it doesn't fit, you can't convict." While the immediate reference was to a glove found behind Simpson's house, the inference was to all the evidence in the case.

If nothing comes to your mind immediately, don't worry. Song writers can spend months finding the right way to express something. As a result, we merely hope you will keep the idea of developing something whenever you have a few quiet moments to think.

Here are some more ideas on making body language a part of any word of mouth program you develop for your business:

- The folks at AAMCO, a company specializing in the inspection and installation of car transmissions, have used the same concept in the tag line of all of their radio and television commercials for years. The first two letters—AA—are always pronounced "Double A" and are followed by the beep beep sound of a car horn. The car horn is then followed by the rest of the spelling—M-C-O. It goes like this: Double A—beep, beep, M-C-O.

  In the same way, Intel always uses a five-note chime (one quarter note followed by four eighth notes) to highlight the fact that its semiconductor chips are used in the product being advertised.

  Even people who never saw the original TV program *Dragnet* are familiar with its rhythmic musical theme—*Dum da dum dum*—to highlight some dramatic moment in the script.

- Hand movements are always a terrific way to incorporate body language into word of mouth advertising. Here is one example. Our publishers have a book on the market called *Power and Price*...it is a serious study about how the prices we pay for the goods and services we need have little to do with the traditional concept of supply and demand. We have suggested that every time someone mentions the book to an audience of any number the name be emphasized by an accompanying ritual: The fist of one hand being pounded into the palm of the other while saying POWER, followed immediately by a dollar sign being traced in the air as the second half of the title—PRICE—is articulated. See that ritual a few times and the linkage between a corporation's power in the marketplace and the prices charged for their goods and services can get set in stone.

If nothing else comes to mind, we always recommend that a hand be formed into a telescope shape—to emphasize focusing on a particular product or service—while relating the movement to the name you want people to remember.

- Advertising agencies know the value of visually tying a movement to a point to remember. The next time you are watching television, note the number of commercials that show someone pointing, holding their thumb up, waving a flag, smiling, or otherwise linking a positive physical gesture to a name or slogan as part of the last image seen on the commercial.

  Such positive physical gestures are often seen to good advantage in political campaigns. Remember how supporters of Corazon Aquino made the shape of a "C" with their thumb and index finger to signal their approval of her effort to succeed Ferdinand Marcos, the corrupt president of the Philippines? In fact, it was so effective that government agents were said to be behind several well publicized thumb amputations as a way to graphically discourage further use of the sign—and by implication, further support for Mrs. Aquino.

  Less dangerously, but equally pointedly, supporters of George W. Bush's 2000 presidential campaign in the United States raised their three middle fingers to create a rough letter "W" in a salute to the middle name of the man they wanted to differentiate from his father. Seeing 20,000 people at a rally signaling in unison with their hands in this way seemed to resonate far more strongly with television viewers than the sounds of cheering or the sight of a red, white, and blue balloon drop.

Of course, Texans are comfortable with hand signals. They raise their index finger and pinky to imitate the distinctive widespread horns of a Texas longhorn steer, the mascot of the University of Texas.

- In terms of other forms of body language, voice cues are vital—especially on the telephone. Bored, negative, and dull tones are an automatic turnoff, whatever the caller is selling.

  A few years ago we consulted with a group in England called Programs Ltd. One of their divisions was involved in telemarketing. They used to conduct a few minutes of exercise before the calling began to get everyone ready for a day on the telephone. The exercises required no skill and no sweat, just some purposeful moving around, waving the arms, bending the legs, and vocalizing a few sounds to get the burrs out of the voice. Silly? To visitors, perhaps, but to the employees no.

  The physical effort got their blood moving and that got more oxygen into their systems, which gave them more energy for their tasks. They felt better, and feeling better was conveyed in their telephone voices. We do the same thing all the time ourselves. Whenever we have a call involving a sale, we make sure we rehearse the opening line or two to be sure to be sounding up, cheerful, bright, and energetic; if we have a radio interview to do by telephone, we always count out loud to ten to make sure our voice is strong, our energy is high, and our happiness is apparent. If we are cheerful, the listener is sure to catch the fever as well.

- But word of mouth is about third-party communication. It is usually a happy customer telling a friend about something the customer has enjoyed. How do you get a customer to use positive body language, including voice cues, when talking about your product or service? While a slogan or name linked to a particular sound or gesture works and can be duplicated over the Internet as well as in traditional ads, it is difficult for small companies to establish.

The best way we know for smaller companies to get customers to exhibit positive word of mouth comments is to do something that genuinely creates its own excitement—to do something that so surprises and delights the customer by its novelty, its generosity, or its quality that the customer will *want* to share it with others.

It happened to us some 30 years ago in Panama. Before leaving Los Angeles, we had purchased a brand new Hewlett-Packard business calculator that had a number of new exclusive features. One evening I was on my own, so I decided to take the instruction booklet to a restaurant to practice with the machine while waiting to be served.

> After a while we were able to master how to get the machine to calculate the number of days between two dates. We were so amazed at the speed of this feature that we asked others—total strangers—in this very nice restaurant to tell us the dates of their birth. We wanted to tell them the exact number of days they had lived to share with their kids. It seems almost embarrassing now to recall that evening, but at that time we were all so dazzled by the technology that I am sure I sold several machines for Hewlett-Packard without knowing it and without, of course, receiving a commission.
>
> It is a good example of trying to generate enough excitement in the customer that he or she will automatically convey enthusiasm, support, and encouragement for a product, service, or business, not only by the words employed but by the tone of voice and physical movements used to describe the item in question.

The point is the same one we always make about word of mouth advertising: Be creative, be original, be daring; in short, do anything that is re-MARK-able—an activity that is truly worth describing and discussing—and people will spontaneously and enthusiastically talk about you and your product! It is the same message we deliver about body language: Be bold, be broad, be different. When daring words and different body language come together, they can make a memorable impact.

Finally, if nothing else, use a made-up word to describe your product, service, or event. These words are always fun, evoke a smile, and can link, by their strange sound, specific body language to a new addition to someone's vocabulary. We have used:

- AUTOMAGIC
- FANTASTERRIFIC
- GINORMOUS
- MAJORTASTIC
- SPECIALOSITY

in projects we have undertaken for clients. They work. We invite you to apply them—or others of your own invention—to the goods and services you are selling.

MORE PRACTICE

MORE PRACTICE

OK. Enough explaining on our part, Now it's time for you to exhibit a little more of your skills at conveying meaning through body language.

Many believe that the eyes offer a window on our souls. Watch the eyes of someone you are talking to and you will know what that person is thinking. Not quite true according to the experts, but the idea is on the right track. In actuality, the eyes themselves are not doing much; rather it is the whole panoply of movements *surrounding* the eyes that goes into motion. These movements may involve the eyebrows, the eyelids, the cheeks, a person's brow and/or mouth. Taken together and in an infinite number of possible configurations, these facial features focused around the eyes accurately convey an enormous range of emotions.

Because we are about to ask you to practice facial expressions that you can monitor in a mirror, these exercises are better done when you are home, at the office, or even perhaps stuck in traffic somewhere. If you do happen to be caught in traffic, you can tilt the rearview mirror toward you to watch yourself. Just be sure to reset the mirror whenever the traffic begins to move again.

Here is the technique. We will give you a description of a facial expression we want you to adopt. Before putting the muscles in your face to work, it is best to get a vision in your mind of what a person looks like when feeling the emotion encompassed by the expression. If you cannot think of a person, think of an event that might cause you to have that emotion. Just as soon as you have that mental vision, put on the face and glance at yourself in the mirror. If it doesn't come out quite like you want it, work on a more vivid picture in your mind before trying again.

OK. Here we go:

- *We want your face to register...SURPRISE!*

Did your eyebrows arch, your brow furrow, and your eyes open wide?

- *OK, let's try SHOCK!*

Did your eyes, brow, and eyebrows do almost the same thing, but this time with your mouth turning down? Did you notice how just tiny changes in muscles movements seem to make all the difference in what is being conveyed in a facial expression?

- *Now show PLEASURE!*

Was everything about the same again, but didn't your mouth turn up in a little smile?

- *Finally, show yourself looking ANNOYED!*

Didn't your mouth flatten to a straight line and your eyebrows lower as your eyes became narrow slits?

It isn't likely that you needed lessons in recognizing the meaning of these facial expressions, but it is good to practice how to manipulate your own face into subtle changes to convey specific messages by nonverbal means. It may not reinforce what you are saying, but it avoids the Clintonesque ambiguity that causes confusion in others when body movements and words do not seem to match. Here is a story that emphasizes that point.

Drive down Sunset Boulevard in Los Angeles any day of the year and you will see people selling maps purportedly showing where the homes of television and movie stars are located in Beverly Hills. My brother, now a senior partner in a law firm, worked this job one summer in the 1950s. He was told to wear a colorful hat to draw instant attention (he chose a cricketer's cap), make eye contact with the drivers as they approached his position, and then wave them toward the curb in an encouraging and friendly manner. It worked then and it continues to work today.

Those who seem to communicate with the passing traffic through their friendly manner, are reeling in the cars, hard pressed during tourist season to find enough time to show the map's features and collect the appropriate payment. Then there are those selling maps who really seem to wish themselves doing something else. They are walking in tight circles, standing like lamp posts, or slouched in a lawn chair sometimes appearing to doze off, sometimes staring into space, sometimes talking with friends. All of these tend to get little action. The difference is obvious. Those who are animated and cheerful, wave and smile, seem to get the desired response and the business. It is a strong endorsement for finding ways to use unambiguous body language as part of a comprehensive selling programs.

An example of the power of body language to convey meaning that others can readily understand came from the same brother. In fact, being shy and usually withdrawn, he found that expressing himself through body language was sometimes easier than using words to convey the same meaning.

I once went with him to visit a mutual client in the hospital. We could not get there during posted visiting hours, but he told me not to worry. Walk through those halls as if you belong—in other words like a doctor on the staff seeking out a patient's room—and no one will say a word to you. As we were both dressed in suits, no one gave us a second glance. We marched through the hospital and reached our client's room without challenge. On the way, my brother taught me to ignore the close-in room numbers and corridor signs—a dead giveaway that we didn't know the way and might not belong—and focus our gaze at the information on the walls and hanging from the ceilings at some distance.

The same body language works for me every time I go somewhere, particularly to those places where I might not have the proper credentials or the proper permissions. I use it at convention centers when a show is not yet open to the public, in hotel lobbies where I want to use a restroom, and at conferences when we want to hear someone speak but might lack a ticket.

As you have realized by now, we take a very broad view of body language, believing it encompasses all methods of communication. For example, tone of voice is crucial to all spoken language and becomes, in our view, a form of body language when an individual cannot be seen or does not speak the dominant language of the area.

Let me give you an example. I was in Vienna recently and was having breakfast in the hotel's dining room. Each table was equipped with a large carafe of coffee, but tea was not in sight. I waved at a waitress and in my most courteous voice said in English: "Do you think I might have a cup of tea?" All I got was a blank stare of confusion.

Being in Vienna, I was instantly reminded of the play *Amadeus* where the emperor, after listening to a performance of one of Mozart's newest compositions, proclaimed to his court that he thought there were too many notes. I was guilty of putting too many *words* into my question. Had I merely asked for "Tea?"—accompanied by the appropriate body language of eyes wide and eyebrows arched to signal a question—I know I would have been brought what I wanted without any confusion and without any delay on anyone's part.

The same point is made in a recent television ad for voice activated electronic equipment found in a particular brand of luxury car. The actor playing the part of a confident executive inserts his key in the ignition and barks "CD," followed quickly by "lights." With that, the sound system springs to life and the headlights pop on. The message seems to be the same one taught by the military: Leadership works best when commands are simple and clear.

Let's now pretend that *you* are in a foreign country and need to find the closest taxi stand. Explain out loud to yourself the combined spoken and unspoken language you might use to get this information.

How did it go? What gestures and/or words did you use?

We had to solve this very problem ourselves in Warsaw a few years back as we came out of a department store. We said "TAXI?" to the first person we encountered on the street, accompanying our question with our eyes wide and our arms pantomiming the manipulation of a car's steering wheel. A nice man on the street pointed us toward an intersection. When we got there, we saw no taxis but repeated the word and gesture. A second individual indicated that we had to go another block and then turn left. When we followed these signed directions, we found five taxis waiting for customers.

To show you once again how important the *combination* of verbal and nonverbal communication is, here is a telephone experiment. Pretend you are a salesperson who has been told to call a Mrs. Marion Lee at her office. She is interested in buying a new piano from you. To establish the proper attitude, you fix in your mind that you want to sound very bright and cheerful when the phone is answered. You punch in the numbers and a receptionist barks back: "Law Offices!" You say: "Mrs. Lee, please."

Now try this same scene in front of a mirror. Did you notice that in your effort to sound bright and cheerful that your eyes went wide and your eyebrows arched as you asked for Mrs. Lee? While in this case the body language *followed* the attitude you wanted to convey, the opposite is also true. If you first adopt the body language, you will have no trouble finding the right tone of voice for the attitude you want to present.

Try it with this scenario. Mr. William Freeman owes you a small amount of money. He had promised to call you back after checking with his bookkeeper, but he did not. You are a little uptight that you have to chase him. So you want the right tone in your voice when you talk to him...not angry but *annoyed* that you cannot get this small debt resolved without a lot of effort. Put your face into an expression of exasperation or mild annoyance, then pretend to ask for Mr. Freeman when a mythical receptionist answers the phone.

Were your lips pinched, your brow lightly furrowed, and your eyes peering through slits formed by your narrowed eyelids? That kind of look can certainly put the right amount of asperity in your tone of voice as you start a conversation.

Remember to use any of these movements you have practiced the next time you need to add a little "body language" to add impact to your verbal statements.

ON THE INTERNET

ON THE INTERNET

Now let us turn to what may be the hottest form of marketing today...e-sales. While we believe that word of mouth can be particularly effective as an Internet form of promotion, can body language be applied to selling on the Internet as well?

It seems almost contradictory to think that individual physical gestures can be projected through the movement of anonymous electrons, but, yes, we think the spirit of body language can be applied to the World Wide Web. Here are some ideas how this can be accomplished:

- As we have learned, body language is very good at expressing feelings—true feelings. Very often how a person *actually* feels is more accurately expressed through an involuntary gesture or particular movement than in carefully chosen words.

  So when you are writing something in an EMail or for a Web page, try expressing things that would reflect your body language if you were dealing with someone *in person*. If something has you excited, say: "I am literally ***jumping*** up and down about this." Or if something seems innovative, try: "This new product is sure to ***point*** the way." To further emphasize the body language element in your written communication, you can put the words *jumping* and *point*, as we did above, in ***BOLD ITALICS***.

- Because so many people are adept at attaching photos and even video to their EMail or posting all kinds of illustrations on their own Web sites, the opportunity to express aspects of body language and *show* it should become a part of the way you communicate on the Internet.
- Of course, the techies have been way ahead on the question of computers and body language. Almost as soon as EMail became popular in the mid-1990s, a whole language of keyboard symbols arose to express emotions in the same kind of shorthand that a shrug, a wink, or a wave can produce. The keyboard symbols are called "emoticons."We would guess that few today draw a blank when they see a full colon followed by a closed parenthesis—:)—at the end of an EMail message. This is the accepted way to express happiness. I know that when we see it in an EMail message, we always smile at the extra effort the writer took to emphasize his or her feelings. It is also an indication of our fondness for those who believe in the fullness of communication. Here are some other emoticons you may want to adopt in your written communication:

  :@ - Shock.
  :(- Sadness, unhappiness.
  :I - Indifference—the equivalent of a shrug of the shoulders.
  :Q - Confusion; a raise of the eyebrows.
  :O - Surprise or the realization of an error (the equivalent of "uh oh!").

- Use of various keyboard symbols is not limited to these types of specialized symbols. All kinds of emotions can be expressed by merely manipulating the keys themselves. We show annoyance or anger by using CAPITAL LETTERS. Techies have long interpreted capital letters as the written equivalent of verbal SHOUTING. Either way, the CAPITALS make the wanted point.

  We have a Swedish colleague who puts emphasis into her EMails and faxes by overloading the ends of sentences with exclamation points (!!!) and question marks (???), sometimes putting them together in wild combinations (exclamation point, exclamation point, question mark, question mark, question mark, question mark, exclamation point, exclamation point, exclamation point—!!????!!!) to be sure the reader gets her emphasis. We, ourselves, use a lot of dots (...) and dashes (—) in all of our written communication to indicate what verbal speech can produce by a pause, change of tone, and the like.

This effort to make written communication as effective as person-to-person conversation is reminiscent of the importance of salons in 17th and 18th century Vienna. There, conversation became the principal medium through which new ideas were exchanged and social developments assessed. In fact, conversation as a means of entertainment and enlightenment became so important that letters were written by traveling participants with the intent that they be *read* aloud on behalf of their absent authors.

Today, the *art* of conversation has almost been lost to an avalanche of other forms of communication and certainly does not score on the modern list of favorite types of entertainment. In fact, *The Wall Street Journal* reported on a Silicon Valley version of the famous Viennese salons and cafes. In California, people are consciously gathering regularly for food and issue discussion precisely to go off-line and to get connected face-to-face with other human beings—to inform, to learn, to influence, to impress, and to amuse.

MORE BUSINESS SITUATIONS

MORE BUSINESS SITUATIONS

Here is another example of how a salesman used basic body language to his advantage with new clients.

> *The salesman was of Lebanese background, working for a Geneva-based mutual fund distributor called Investors Overseas Services. I met this man in Ecuador in the 1960s, and he told me his favorite opening gambit whenever meeting a prospective client for the first time. He would enter the individual's office and as he approached the person, he would withdraw his business card from a suit pocket. In his effort to present the card, he would purposely fumble it. As the card fluttered toward the carpet, he said that inevitably the new client would automatically stoop down to retrieve it to avoid embarrassment to his visitor. As the salesman apologized for his clumsiness, he would be sure to hook his hand under the prospective client's elbow to gently help him back to an erect posture after the client had retrieved the card.*
>
> *In that moment and in that innocuous touch, the initial roles of the two people would be subtly reversed. The prospective client would be psychologically cast into a subservient position—someone adopting a lower posture, doing a menial task, or in need of help—and the salesman would instantly assume a dominant, even protective status of someone standing tall while providing assistance. The salesman said that after this little tableau was played out, there was never any resistance to the ensuing sales presen-*

> *tation; the prospective client listened with respect and accepted the salesman as a figure of authority on the topic at hand—international finances.*

The salesman also pointed out to me that, for obvious reasons, he could use the trick only once and that he had to be sure that he never used it when there were others in the room—for fear of repeating it before someone who had already experienced it and to avoid two prospects going for the dropped card simultaneously. He further pointed out that not every initial presentation resulted in a sale—bad timing, lack of funds, other priorities, and a host of other typical excuses sometimes prevented him from closing the sale on a first visit. But he also noted that the body language brought the subsequent relationship between the two men onto an equal basis that made closing easier

So the next time you need an equalizer in a conversation at a cocktail party, in an office, or anywhere else, think about dropping something to see the kind of response you achieve and the good you can do for yourself thereafter.

By the way, we have all seen this same type of blatant body language in the animal world. Amphibians and reptiles make peace by lowering themselves to the ground in an act of submission. Small dogs get their heads below their shoulders and often roll onto their backs to demonstrate that they pose no threat to a larger animal with which they come into contact.

Robin Dunbar observed other such behavior in baboons: An older female was being bugged by two younger males. Having had enough of them, he notes, she "...stare[d] meaningfully at the two juveniles, her head lowered and her eyebrows raised..." The juveniles got the message. She was displaying anger and the threat of physical punishment. They soon scampered off to interact with other animals in the compound.

Even something as innocent as whiskers—an important source of sensory information for cats as they move about—are also used to communicate information to other cats. Interestingly, these tactile hairs tend to be twice as thick, have roots three times as deep, and are surrounded by a host of nerves and blood vessels. Because of this, a breath of air or the slightest movement is sufficient to provide key information to a cat through the whiskers.

The next time you have a chance to observe a cat, note the position of its whiskers. If they are pushed forward, they are suggesting friendliness and curiosity. But according to the head of Cornell University's Feline Health Center, when they are pulled back flat against the cheek, a cat is signalling aggressiveness and / or hostility to something around it.

Here is another interesting use of body language to achieve a specific business end. *The Wall Street Journal* reports that a media consultant was pecking away on his laptop on a flight from San Francisco when he sensed another pair of eyes intently looking at his computer screen. The consultant had experienced this before. So he swung into action. With just a few keystrokes, he opened a file called READTHIS. Up popped a single sentence:

If you can read this,
you ought to be ashamed of yourself.

The traveler next to him physically stiffened. "It works every time," said the consultant. "It's a nice, polite two-by-four between the eyes."

Here are some other common body language signals. As you hear each described, take a moment to indicate what you think these movements and gestures might mean before reading the explanation:

- *A line of men holding their hands chest high with their palms open and pointed upwards.*

It is the typical supplication of a Muslim in prayer; Christians, on the other hand, bring their hands together gently and point the tips of their fingers upward. It is the same use of body language, just slightly different gestures to get to the same end.

- *A man in a group of people, gathered around a professional golfer deciding on his next shot, suddenly pushes his way to the front of the crowd, then thrusts a hand into his pocket. He looks worried as his eyes dart from the golfer to the officials on the fringes of the players to the people surrounding him.*

While context is always important, plainclothes bodyguards assigned to protect professional golfers at tournaments decided that this guy was not looking for the closest Port-a-Potty. As they started to move closer, the guy panicked and tried to back out of the crowd. After wrestling him to the ground, they found he was carrying a loaded handgun while following Tiger Woods around a golf course in Phoenix.

- *An accomplished actor delivers his most telling lines by leaning the upper half of his body forward toward the intended recipient of his remark.*

It turns out that Alan Alda is a master of this technique. Watch him, then emulate him. If you want to make a point emphatically without raising your voice or waving your arms, just try leaning in at the waist to get closer to your listener's face. You'll notice the impression you make instantly.

- *A Japanese woman has invited an American visitor to her home. She is waiting for him on the porch. As he approaches, she places both of her palms on her legs just above the knees and bows very deeply at the waist.*

The traditional bow as practiced by the Japanese is a sign of nonaggression between two individuals. Westerners signal the same nonaggression by shaking hands or waving—a highly stylized gesture that probably had its origins in showing the other person that no weapon was being carried at the ready.

While we can vary a handshake to show different levels of pleasure or familiarity at the time of greeting—strong grip, extra movement up and down, holding on longer than would seem normal—the Japanese have made bowing into an entire art form of subtle communication. For example, who initiates the bow, its depth, and the position of the hands at the time the bow is executed indicates the relative social standing of the two individuals and/or the willingness of one individual to submit to the will of the other.

FINAL EXAMINATION

FINAL EXAMINATION

Before putting you through a dress rehearsal of how well you can produce or interpret body language, let us turn to yet another proof of its importance as a means of communication. This time the proof has to do with recent research into electoral politics. What seems to count most among voters is not the policy statements of candidates or the issues they claim to care most about but the first impression they make. Like jungle animals who decide with one quick look whether to flee, fight, or bond with another creature, so voters tend to respond with a primal instinct based on physical appearance and body language.

So crucial is physical appearance and body language to electoral success that a group of Northern Illinois University students were able to correctly predict the top vote getters among the 16 candidates in the 1996 *Romanian* elections! They accomplished this feat by merely looking at some video clips and still photographs of the candidates in action. As Professor James Schubert points out: "The emotion[al response] happens first. [We] make up the reasons for it later."

Just one example of how this works: Political psychologists say that facial features—the set of the nose, the appearance of the cheekbones, the status of a person's hair—have been associated from time immemorial with high levels of testosterone and strong immune systems in males. To prove the point, the psychologists asked a test audience to concentrate on these characteristics in photographs of West Point cadets, then select those cadets most likely to have risen to the rank of general officer. Responding to what appears to be deeply imbedded triggers that tell us who have the "best genes," a vast majority of the test audience correctly selected those who in fact had achieved general officer rank.

In short, the oft repeated chant from political pundits and candidates that voters truly care more about issues and character than personality and looks is probably totally wrong. In the end, voters only really seem to care about how a candidate strikes them personally and subjectively the first time they pay attention to the field!

Now we have two more sets of exercises that test your newly learned skills at producing and interpreting body language. In the first set we want you to produce the body language to pass a message:

- *You are at a conference and you are trying very hard to concentrate on what the presenter is saying. The person behind you has not stopped talking since she sat down. She is oblivious to the fact that the presentation has begun and continues to talk to the person sitting next to her. You need to stop the chatter without disturbing anyone else. What kind of body language might do the trick?*

Did you decide on the age old signal—simply holding an index finger in front of your lips—or did you go for a more emphatic version—eyebrows raised, the finger in front of the lips, and all accompanied by a loud shushing sound?

- *You are at a wedding reception and a very interesting-looking lady is waiting patiently at the other end of the bar for service. You want to get her attention to indicate that you would like to talk with her, but you don't want to lose your place and you certainly don't want to shout the length of the bar at her. What could you do?*

We certainly hope that you resorted to one of the key tricks of flirting—extended eye contact. If you said that you would look in the lady's direction for as long a period of time as necessary—say 6 to 10 seconds or until you caught her eye and then held it, you are on the best track. Once she looked your way, a smile, a nod of the head, a shift of the eye in the direction you will be moving after you get your drink, or any other such signal is strong enough to allow you to approach her to start a conversation.

- *New Yorkers have lately sought ways to signal an apology to other drivers when they have done something in the wrong or when bumping into people while rushing by on a crowded street. We'll tell you what the traffic experts are suggesting after you have had a chance to think of what* you *might do to signal someone else that you are sorry for something you just did.*

The experts suggest a light tap of the palm of your hand to your forehead. It is a gesture that most people might read as indicating that you have done something stupid and you are apologetic.

Fine for the United States and some other countries, perhaps, but not so fine in Mediterranean regions where the same gesture signals "I'm crazy" or the other person is stubborn or thick headed. Dr. David Givens, an anthropologist at the Center for Non-Verbal Studies in Spokane, Washington, offers another suggestion. He notes that the universal signal for feeling contrite or helpless is to hold the hand up with the palm pointing outward. He suggests that by folding the thumb across the open palm, you show four fingers, which the subconscious brain interprets as a sign of weakness. It is meant to convey the message that the person meant no harm by his action.

- *It's around 5:00AM and you're up early. No newspaper yet, but it's due at any moment. You hear a car coming down the street, assume it's the delivery man, and are waiting in your driveway when he slows just enough to toss the paper. How do you signal a thank you to him?*

Two thumbs up would have been one way to show your appreciation. Another good way to signal thank you is to have clapped your hands lightly in front of you. A third and perhaps most universal signal might have been to circle the thumb and forefinger in an OK sign.

- *Finally, a situation that we've all been in—expressing disapproval. This time we want you to imagine that you are in a meeting with your boss accompanied by an ambitious subordinate who has had charge of the project under discussion. You have told the subordinate not to say a word until you invite him to speak and then to speak only to the question posed. But when the boss raises a new topic, you can see that your young colleague is ready to offer a comment. Indicate to your subordinate, in three evermore emphatic steps, to be quiet. The first signal would be a gentle movement reminding him not to talk; the second would be a clear sign to be silent while you respond; and the third would be an absolute directive to shut up.*

As with most of what we have discussed so far, there is really no absolute right or wrong way to use body language to convey information, only *your* own way. The rules are simple: You have to be comfortable with making nonverbal signals and the other person has to clearly understand your meaning. No use for us to suggest something that you would feel awkward in doing or that no one else would understand.

In any case, the three signals *we* might have conveyed are as follows:

1. To remind the other person not to talk, we might have rubbed a hand across our mouth, as if we were wiping away a crumb, before just letting a forefinger appear to bisect the lips as the hand was being withdrawn.

2. When we wanted our young subordinate to desist from responding to the boss, we would use one of the oldest tools in the body language arsenal—a hand laid on the forearm of the other person. You may have seen it used in various television chat shows or even among husbands and wives; it is an almost universal signal for the other person to stop talking instantly and let the speaker continue his thought until completed.

3. Finally, if nothing else worked, we might clear our throat and turn to the subordinate with a long wide-eyed stare with our eyebrows arched high. This should be reminder enough of the admonition given before the meeting began to JUST SHUT UP. If the subordinate missed that signal—or chose to ignore it to try to curry favor with the big boss—he probably should be told to write and sign an undated letter of resignation to be filled in the next time he chooses to ignore you.

The second set of exercises in our mythical final examination deals with *reading* body language exhibited by someone else. Here goes:

- *It is Academy Award night in Hollywood and actress Andy McDowell tells an interviewer that she is relaxed and calm about her chances of winning an Oscar. But the camera catches her thumb rubbing constantly against her forefinger, faster and faster as she relates that she left an expensive necklace on loan from a famous jeweler back at the hotel. She is hoping that someone sent to retrieve it arrives before she has to enter the auditorium. Do you think her words and her body language are in harmony?*

Clearly not. As an actress she could convey calm in an otherwise upsetting situation, but until she learns to control her body language movements as well, she gives away her true feelings.

- *It is a cool night, but you notice the man has opened his coat, is running a finger around his collar, and has his handkerchief out. You ask him what is the matter, thinking he might be sick or worried about something, but he says blandly: "Nothing." You absolutely don't believe him when he adds that everything is fine. What can you do to get at what you perceive to be the truth of the situation?*

A direct confrontation in which you challenge the individual with the evidence of his anxiety might prove the best way to get at what is really bothering him. If that isn't enough to draw the person out, generally asking a leading question should do the trick: "Thinking about business?" "Concerned about the family?" "Worried about dealing with the boss?"

The most important rule to remember when trying to get at the truth in those situations where there is a discrepancy between verbal expressions and nonverbal signals is surprise! Nothing seems to melt the barriers faster than exposing what someone believes is hidden from view. The shock of revelation usually ends all pretense. So when you suspect someone is not telling you the truth, hit him or her with your observations immediately and directly. Don't be polite, don't be cute, don't delay.

While we have consistently cautioned our listeners to evaluate body language in the context of the situation and the words being spoken, it is interesting to note that detecting untruths is very difficult. In study after study, most people perform at chance levels when asked to determine who is telling a lie and who is telling the truth. The same researchers also found that those most skilled at detecting liars—Secret Service agents, for example—do not rely on a single clue, such as lack of eye contact or constant throat clearing, but on a cluster of verbal and nonverbal signals instead.

CONCLUSION

CONCLUSION

Here then is a brief review of the major points we have made in this book:

1. Nonverbal communication is more than a window into what someone else may be feeling. It is also a crucial means of conveying information when verbal contact becomes impossible.

2. Be as conscious of the signals you may be emitting through your own gestures and movements—those that you intend and those that you make make inadvertently—as you are of what you see other people doing.

3. If you sense an ambiguity between what a person says and what he or she may be indicating through body language, be sure to seek clarification directly and immediately. But do not assume that either the words or the body language is conveying what the person truly feels; you may get it all wrong.

4. Remember that verbal communication has its own ambiguities. Take for example the promise of the mayor of North Platte, Nebraska, to walk naked down the street if the local humane society was able to raise $5000. When they did, the mayor in fact walked a dog named "Naked" down Main Street instead of appearing in the buff as so many assumed.

5. Do not rely on any single gesture or word to determine the true meaning of what is being conveyed; be prepared to put all that you hear and all that you see into *context*.

6. Most of all we urge you to remember the most important lesson of this book:

**IT IS NOT *WHAT* YOU SAY
THAT COUNTS,
BUT *HOW* YOU SAY IT!**

In short, people tend to get much more from what they *see* than from what they *hear*. Of course, this should not be an alien concept to any of us. We have all grown up on the adage that actions speak louder than words!

NOTES

ACKNOLWEDGEMENTS

No book, no matter how original or experienced the author, comes to market without the assistance of a number of other people. The individuals who helped bring *Watch It!*to life are noted below:

Barbara DeKovner-Mayer — Barbara is the author's wife. She introduced him to the whole topic of body language and was instrumental in helping him see the potential meaning behind certain movements and gestures.

Charles Goldman — Chuck has edited many of our books. While he is expert in what he does, he is never dogmatic about the rules of grammar and useage he follows. For example, he points out that style authorities recommend hyphens when the phrase word-of-mouth modifies another word (as in word-of-mouth advertising); but he accepts the fact that the author views the use of hyphens as a denigration of the worth of this type of advertising. Harris notes that traditional media advertising is not hyphenated nor is the term public relations services or product presentations. If word of mouth advertising is fully equal to these three other forms of market promotion, as Harris believes it is, no hyphens should be used. Another point: Goldman prefers e-mail or email; Harris has referred to this type of electronic communication as EMail since the early 1990s when there was no clear guidance on the matter; he has used this formulation in his books *Don't Take Our Word For It!* and *Let Your Fingers Do the Talking*. Retaining the Harris usage, rather than employing the Goldman preference, is for the sake of consistency.

Alan Lister	This old friend from England taught me a lot about business before and after I left the diplomatic service. One of his contributions was the use of made-up words to enhance attention to a product or service. Ginormous, as a synonym for large, was a part of his normal vocabulary and he used the word "automagic," in the name of one of his companies to great effect.
Penelope Morensen	Penny handles most of the administrative tasks for The Americas Group. She kept the project organized for the author and on track to reach market before BookExpo America 2001 where it was introduced.
John Osborne	John designed the cover. John comes from England and operates almost exclusively over the Internet from a firm called NightShiftGraphics. com It is a tribute to the new world of global commerce that such a happy relationship could be established at such a distance without anyone from The Americas Group having met anyone from NightShiftGraphics.
Diane Tupper Sieck	Diane manages a firm called International Artwork in Carmel, California. She is responsible for supervising the creation of the bar graphs that are mandatory today for sales and inventory control. Without her assistance on the proper way to present this arcane element of book publishing, this title would never reach the marketplace.
Michael Stolkey	Michael is a sales representative for Fidlar Doubleday, a firm in Michigan that provides print-on-demand services to publishers. This brave new world is changing the way books are printed and distributed. This is the third title printed in this way by The Americas Group. Working with Mike and his colleagues is a delight.

BIBLIOGRAPHY

As was noted at the outset, this book is an extension of several others written by the author on word of mouth advertising. As such, it was designed principally as an aid to understanding how important body language is to the impact of word of mouth commentary. It is appropriate then to give credit to the work of others who contributed greatly to this effort.

Robin Dunbar, *Evolution of Language,* Faber and Faber Limited, 1996

Julia Fast, *Body Language,* MJF Books, 1970

Godfrey Harris and Greg Harris, *Talk Is Cheap,* The Americas Group, 1991

Godfrey Harris and Greg Harris, *How to Generate Word of Mouth Advertising,* The Americas Group, 1995

Godfrey Harris, *Don't Take Our Word For It!,* The Americas Group, 1998

Godfrey Harris and Barbara D. Mayer, *From Trash to Treasure,* The Americas Group, 1983

Godfrey Harirs, *Talk Is Easy,* The Americas Group, 1999

Godfrey Harris, *Let Your Fingers Do the Talking,* The Americas Group, 2000

Gerard I Nierenberg and Henry Calero, *How to Read a Person Like a Book,* Barnes and Noble Books, 1993

George Stephanopoulous, *All Too Human,* Little Brown and Company, 1999

Tom Wolfe, *A Man In Full,* Farrar Straus Gioroux, 1998

INDEX

MEET THE AUTHOR OF *WATCH IT!*

GODFREY HARRIS has been a public policy consultant based in Los Angeles, California, since 1968. He began consulting after short careers as a university lecturer, U.S. Army intelligence officer, foreign service officer with the Department of State, and organizational specialist in the President's Executive Office.

As President of Harris/Ragan Management Group, he has focused the firm's activities on projects that offer alternative solutions to matters of community concern. In fulfilling that role, he has specialized in political and economic analysis; marketing public and private sector services through word of mouth advertising; developing new environmental products; creating commemorative events; and promoting international tourism.

This is the 28th book he has written or co-authored. He holds degrees from Stanford University and the University of California, Los Angeles.